TELL ME WHAT YOU THINK

Which is your favorite recipe?
What surprised you about this book?
Did you find something that needs correction?
Want to share your thoughts or just say "Hello"?

Contact the author at
djkennebeck@emmaus-way.com

Other books by D.J. Kennebeck
can be found at emmaus-way.com/shop

Also by D.J. Kennebeck:

The Pivotal Pastor
ISBN 979-8-9866668-0-8
Remembering Ron Lewinski
ISBN 979-8-9866668-7-7

ROSA'S LITTLE BOOK OF RECIPES

D. J. KENNEBECK

EMMAUS WAY LLC

ISBN: 979-8-9866668-1-5 (Paperback)

Cover and book design by David J. Kennebeck
The manuscript for this book was prepared using Scrivener.
Photographs are from family archives. Some photos were taken by a professional photographer. No copyright infringement is intended. I do not own nor claim to own the rights to any of the professionally produced photos in this book.

Published by Emmaus Way LLC.
Printed in the U.S.A

First Print Edition 2024
10 11 12 1 2 **3** 240312

To Mom, with thanks for many things.

Homestead of the parents of Henry, Rosa's husband
(1940)

Dear relative or friend,

Rosa was my mother. She was a good cook and baker, the best mom she could be. At some point, she wrote several recipes in a spiral notebook. She passed in 1983. I don't recall how or when her notes came into my possession. But clearly, she wanted to share her knowledge. So, I am continuing what she began over half a century ago.

This book also acknowledges my parent's 100th wedding anniversary in 2023. My father (Henry) was born in 1896; my mother (Rosa) in 1902. My brother (Vernon) and sister (Elvera) came in 1924 and 1928, respectively. I arrived in 1945 and was thus raised as an only child. This spared me the sibling rivalry about who gets the last cookie or the first piece of the pie.

My decision to preserve memories is also a nod to people's efforts to live their lives and raise their families. "Family" is undervalued too often today. Each generation is challenged to discover life anew. Any absence of family life makes that process burdensome. I cannot view the photos in this collection without wondering about the paths of these people's lives. As a child, I regarded many adults as 'old' people. Looking back, I now realize several individuals were only in their thirties and forties.

Most came from working farms. My brother's generation, one before mine, transitioned away from farming. He left the Illinois plains to travel the Pacific Ocean with the U.S. Navy during World War II. After being discharged in San Diego, he married and raised his family in California. My sister became a housewife, raising her family in towns near our northern Illinois homestead. Both my siblings had three children.

My childhood memories associate food with family and friends. So, I've included recipes and people's pictures in this collection. Preparing and consuming these dishes invokes images of people and the remembrances they formed.

Most of my cousins lived on farms; the rest of the family were "townfolk." Weekend gatherings provided a work/life balance for both. Sunday was a day of rest, except for certain farm chores. Adults played yard games like horseshoes and croquet during the summer and cards inside during the winter. I had a knack for winning at Canasta despite having to grasp a literal handful of cards.

Summer called for an iced refreshment — lemonade or root beer — on a hot day. I recall the pungent odor of beer — the adult version — spilled on the lawn. The yeasty fumes were both appealing and repulsive. Odds are the beer was Pabst Blue Ribbon, Hamms, or Schlitz. "What'll you have?" "From the land of sky-blue waters." "When you're out of Schlitz, you're out of beer." The breweries had effective TV marketing. I knew their slogans long before I grew old enough to consume their product legally.

I can hear the solid clang of a metal horseshoe striking a firmly grounded rod. A ringer. It is followed by howls of joy and disappointment from the two opposing players and their supporters. Nearby, a circle of wives in their white wooden lawn chairs object to the sudden outburst. They reprimand the men to "shush" before resuming their cackle of gossip and criticism between sips of lemonade. I detect the alluring aroma of sweet corn in the husk roasting over a charcoal pit. It is soon dipped in butter, salted, and ravished. I could have consumed more, except good manners (as the neighbor's guest) dictated I refrain.

Nearby is a "sandbox" made from a large tractor tire placed on flat ground and covered with plywood when not in use. The timber kept the gritty sand from becoming sodden during a thunderstorm. It was also a preventive measure against infestation by unwanted playmates such as garter snakes and Daddy-Longlegs. Most importantly, it deterred any wandering cats that might view the sand as a natural attraction and leave behind a disagreeable discovery for our next sandcastle-building session. Sometimes our time in that play space was followed by slurping a root beer float and spinning atop stools at a local soda fountain. There are advantages to living in town as opposed to the country.

Semi-transparent ribbons of silvery smoke swirl in the cool autumn air. A woody scent arises from a two-foot-high pile of crisp brown, orange, and yellow leaves. Smoldering embers soon reduce the colorful pyre to grey ash. No one imagined we were on the threshold of contributing to what they would later debate as "climate change."

There was the enigmatic allure of a "garbage dump" on a relative's farmland. Such private dumps were the forerunners of today's public landfills. A large pit had been dug, into which family — and sometimes friends — discarded things like ice boxes (being replaced by refrigerators). These forsaken possessions formed a three-dimensional puzzle that my youthful eyes scrutinized. The variety of items provided imaginative insights into the lives of the former unidentified owners. Certain objects invited more examination, affirming the proverb that one man's junk is another's treasure.

An ice cream stand was between our house and that junk pit. Riding between them in the bed of the neighbor's pickup truck added to the fun. Seatbelt requirements and rules for passenger safety were more than a decade away. As an invention on the road of perceived progress toward consumer safety, "rules" removed some enjoyment from life. But the delight of stopping for a cone — two scoops, please — on the journey home has not changed.

I recall roller skating on the sidewalk on hot summer days is a great way to develop a thirst for an icy glass of lemonade. The real thing — made from cold water, sugar, and lemons. Back then, people didn't need to rush things or risk disappointment by using a powdered store-bought mixture. The technique for fastening a "skate" (four wheels on a flat metal plate) involved cranking a clamp that gripped the sole of my shoe and lacing a strap across my foot. Being too loose led to losing the wheels and incurring a knee-scraping. Too tight and my feet sent a painful message to my brain. Lemonade washed away discomfort.

The circle of life manifested itself in many ways. One sunny day, a large snapping turtle fatefully tried to cross the highway in front of our house at the wrong time. Watching the foot-long shelled animal being repeatedly run over by a neighbor's car imprinted the event in my memory. I suspect I politely rejected the terrapin soup served that evening. This now seems ironic. My older and more traveled brother eventually introduced me to delicacies such as escargot, tender frog legs, fried calamari, and abalone steaks. I discovered I like them all.

The aroma and muffled explosions of popcorn kernels within a covered kettle over our stove's gas flame teased my ears and nose. Then, my self-control was further tested while sprinkling the warm maize puffs with melted yellow butter and salt. Of course, a new technology called "television" became the latest justification for indulging in this treat. Everyone could afford popcorn, but we were not affluent enough to buy a color TV. Still, the treat (even with 1959's introduction of Jiffy Pop) tasted better while watching television. It felt like being at the movie house (theater) but in the comfort of your home.

Those old TV sets had what I see as two advantages. First, a limited choice of stations (four or five, depending on the distance between you and the transmitter). Second, only two controls: one for volume and the other to select a channel. Locating the desired show was an effortless twist of the dial in contrast to the multitude of buttons and many channels available today. Using a phone as a remote control for TV was the stuff of science fiction. Chester Gould (1900-1985) — creator of the comic strip character Dick Tracy — resided in a nearby town where several cousins lived. An early step toward making Tracy's wristwatch a reality was the transistor radio. The battery-powered device made it easy to listen to sportscaster Jack Brickhouse in my backyard. He'd "take me out to the ball game" with the ever-hopeful Chicago Cubs. I sat in the shade, sipping a cold soda from a bottle worth two cents when returned.

In my early years, we lived outside the town's edge. Cornfields surrounded the house on three sides. The crops became feed for the dairy cows and local farmer's market. The silage had, like beer, a distinct but not repulsive odor. They stored the fodder in a silo next to a barn, making it convenient to shovel the food into the barn. The cattle stalls had a trough in front for feed and water and a trough at the rear to catch waste. I soon learned the wisdom of checking the animal's underbelly before attempting to milk it.

I didn't know at the time that my mother's hometown, Spring Grove, is credited with introducing the tower grain silo. This happened when my mom's mother was born, shortly after the Civil War. By the mid-twentieth century, these agricultural storage units had reached nearly half a million nationwide.

The barn's spacious ground level was a garage for tractors and farm equipment. Gasoline and oil odors escaped from stains in the rough wooden planks beneath the machinery. Inventing play spaces from hay bundles in the overhead loft was a fun activity, but the bales caused considerable itchiness. A warm, sudsy bath with an Ivory soap bar before dinner became a welcome remedy.

As a town dweller with many farming relatives, I'd spend a week on a cousin's farm in the summer. It was the best fun and hardest work of my youth. Throughout my life, I remained convinced every kid should have that experience. There is nothing like living in a different environment to help someone realize there's more to the world than that to which they're accustomed.

Sunday was a time of rituals. First, a breakfast including eggs, bacon, and hash browns. Next, a morning church service. Then, while Mom made lunch, I watched hokey episodes of heroic Flash Gordon battling evil Ming the Merciless. The remaining portion of the day was dedicated to visiting relatives, often lasting past supper. Our gatherings included both town folk and farming families.

Most had children my age to play with, except one couple with only a grandfather clock. I sat in their dim and musty living room, listening to the adults' ramblings. They spoke the native language of our German ancestors. I never revealed that I could understand "enough" of it, such as "dummkopf," and another less flattering kind of "kopf."

I hear the vintage clock tick off the seconds. The pendulum has a hypnotic rhythm lulling me to sleep, only to be abruptly awakened by chimes on the quarter hour. I thought it a cruel contraption to subject a bored youngster to. However, it was no stranger than a peculiarity of our host. He had one glass eye. That wasn't the eccentricity. He augmented his beer by breaking a raw egg into the glass mug. He was the only relative I recall who smoked a pipe. The sweet cherry tobacco aroma was the most pleasant thing about our visits and elevated my assessment of him compared to his cigarette-smoking counterparts.

Our country property was barely large enough to keep a poultry coop. It was a tiny wooden cabin within a fenced dirt yard. Inside the little shed were shelves where the hens could roost and lay eggs. The chickens seemed oblivious to the disagreeable odor within the cramped space. Our feathered friends provided fresh eggs (the most common ingredient in these recipes). Sometimes they themselves became a supper entre. As the saying goes, at breakfast, the chicken has contributed (the egg), but the pig (bacon) is committed. Multiple times, I found myself both enchanted and repelled by the spectacle of a chicken being sacrificed. After the axe severed its neck on the chopping block, the chicken's body thrashed across the dirt floor before finally coming to rest.

We cultivated a vegetable patch — a common practice in those days. We benefited from it year-round. In the summer, we picked ripe vegetables from our garden. In the winter, we ate the product of Mom's laborious work, preserving a variety of food. The heat, humidity, and spicy scents from the canning process filled the house. Mom produced many quart and pint jars — a food cornucopia for consumption during the cold midwestern months. I don't recall any "organic" sections in the stores' produce department because everything still was.

Snow rarely fell before Thanksgiving. Once it did, Winter had arrived. We built snowmen and impressive snow forts in the backyard. The best-packing snow pulls itself off the grass. That was the only time I remember seeing the ground during the winter. Naturally, upon returning indoors and changing into dry clothes, I indulged in a mug of hot cocoa with marshmallows. Occasionally, a few more fluffy white treats proved necessary even after the cocoa had been consumed.

Christmas holidays included mom's homemade cookies, a real tree, and, of course, a visit by Santa. But the most exciting part came earlier — the holiday catalogs from Sears Roebuck & Co. and Montgomery Ward. Decades passed before I discovered that the brother of the CEO at Sears was himself the CEO at Ward's. I perused the colorful pages, looking for items that appealed to me. After skipping the sections on kitchen sets and doll houses, I circled one or more things on nearly every page. Although I expected to receive only a few, daydreaming about many brought joy.

In fact, unlike some children who get so many presents that none have any special appeal, I treasured my few. When you receive three gifts, one being a bag of oranges (obviously not solely yours), the other two have greater value. They garnered all my attention and imagination. It is an example of "less is more" or abundance in scarcity. One year, a Slinky became the gift that kept on giving, similar to the newly invented Hula-Hoop that supposedly sold 25 million units in the first few months.[1] Rather than gyrating my hips, I found the plastic loop to be more fun to throw perpendicular to the ground with a reverse spin, causing it to return to me.

Decorating the Christmas tree seemed a laborious undertaking. My parents energized themselves by playing 78 rpm records. The most worn, based on audible scratches, must have been the "Beer Barrel Polka." Some satisfaction came from cutting snowflakes from colored paper folded in quarters. Then the ritual of threading popcorn occurred ("Oops, sorry, guess I pressed too hard; well, I'll just have to eat that kernel.") When we made popcorn balls — slightly larger than a baseball — I learned my hands got sticky from the Karo syrup and it was best not to wait too long before eating them. A few of Mom's especially decorative cookies became ornaments. They

---

[1] https://www.history.com/this-day-in-history/hula-hoop-patented

were a constant temptation to a child who often admired the festive tree. If a cookie ornament disappeared, there could be no doubt why. We had no pets.

Besides tinsel, ornaments, and strung popcorn, we decorated the tree with strings of those strawberry-shaped, different-colored bulbs. We used the same strands each year. The lights just kept working. Soon, however, planned obsolescence arrived. It exhibits itself today in the holiday lights that work when you pack them up but mysteriously don't turn on next year. The principle also applies to household appliances and automobiles. During my childhood, most things were old because they had been built to last. (No doubt a lesson from the Great Depression and two World Wars.) But America's post-war path to prosperity paralleled a one-way route to becoming a throwaway society.

My childhood belief in Santa Claus ended before my ninth Christmas. I was half asleep on the sofa by the tree in the living room, just steps away from our front door. A loud rapping startled me. I bolted to the door, hoping to see Santa as he took off in his sleigh. But, looking through the cold frosted glass, that wasn't what I saw. Instead, there appeared only a shape resembling a man in a winter cap and coat. He was dashing away through the snow toward the road the turtle had never finished crossing. It didn't take much time for me to deduce that it was Uncle Al, who resided with his wife across the highway. That deduction led to a final realization. My disappointment sought refuge in a cookie already dampened by my tears.

Our cluster of four houses, two on each side of the highway, comprised our "family neighborhood." They had built the residences on parcels carved from the farmland. I don't know what financial arrangement transpired, but I suspect my dad's parents granted the land to my father and his brother. The two brothers and their families lived in adjacent houses purchased from Sears for $5,000 each. Not bad for a three-bedroom (counting the attic), one-bath, two-car garage (known as a 3-1-2 these days). I guess my parents also dreamt as they paged through the Sears catalogs.

The basement had a cistern — a large corner enclosed by four concrete walls — to retain rainwater. It was was rerouted during a rainstorm by a manually controlled flap in the downspout outside. A hand pump by the kitchen sink retrieved the water from the basement reservoir. A coal-burning furnace occupied the basement's center to efficiently heat the single-story house above. It faced a small room that received dusty black deposits occasionally during the cold season.

Like most women those days, my mother visited a hairdresser for cuts and perms. The lady ran the business from a room in their basement. They had excavated the hill to create a driveway on that side of the house. The salon was a room in the corner that had an exterior entrance from the driveway. It was next to the garage, which was also in the basement.

The beautician and her husband owned the adjacent empty corner lot. At ten, I was surprised to hear that we had bought that house and were moving into town. The former owners had chosen an uncommon approach to establishing a new residence. They moved a house from somewhere in town onto the empty lot next door. We didn't yet live there then, so I have no memory of the event, but I've never forgotten their house's origin. Nor their little screened "gazebo" with the grill that produced the tasty roasted corn on the cob.

Our backyard in town, like most others, had a section for a garden. Burpee seed envelopes were attached to a stick at the head of the row, identifying the plants until they sprouted. We had an ample supply of vegetables and fruits, a pear and two apple trees, for mom's canning process. There was no chicken coop in town, thus saving us from being regarded as savages by the surrounding townfolk.

The space below the concrete front stairs functioned perfectly as a "fruit cellar." Dark and cool, it sheltered mom's preserves. Multiple shelves held dozens of jars, and I believe Spring often arrived with several of them untouched.

Not everything from the garden reached the cellar or even the house. I discovered I enjoyed eating green peas straight from the pod. The crisp and tasty little spheres didn't need cleaning. They were naturally packaged in consumable portions. Potatoes, onions, tomatoes, lettuce, cabbage, cucumbers, strawberries, watermelons, rhubarb, herbs, and other produce supplied many ingredients for mom's dishes. We picked dandelions and endive from along the country roads.

This humble volume is based on discovering a book of recipes my mother composed. It was a small, 4" x 6" spiral notebook. She numbered the pages, leaving blanks for future entries, and titled each recipe. Although they list the ingredients, some lack instructions and specifics about time, temperature, and mixing methods. I think she regarded them as reminders, assuming her experience of mixing and baking would complete the formula. Refer to the "Notes" page after this section for more information.

My wife was fortunate to be one of five generations in her family living simultaneously. She recalls often making a favorite recipe from her grandmother. The problem was, it just never turned out the same as Grandma's. One day, she had the chance to help Grandma make it. Everything was the same as what my wife always did except for one ingredient that Grandma hadn't written down. Thereafter, my wife's version turned out the way she'd always expected. You may choose to apply some variations to these recipes.

An ingredient I've discovered that can enhance any dish is universal. While taking care to measure the portions and follow the instructions, include a healthy dose of love. It really can make a difference.

Enjoy perusing the recipes. Don't be too quick to judge based on a name. "Sour Cream Pie," for example, may not sound enticing, but it is a cousin to the pecan pie that many people enjoy. I hope when making and enjoying any of these recipes — perhaps with children or grandchildren — you will form good memories of your own.

— D. J. Kennebeck, 2023

NOTES

Traditional page numbers have been omitted.
Instead, the manually assigned page numbers on the recipe
pages are used as references in the Tables of Content (TOC).

The TOC inside the front cover lists contents by page number.
The TOC inside the back cover lists contents by Recipe Name.
To make ingredients easier to manually identify, they have been listed
next to each recipe. If you are reading an ebook version, then you can
use the SEARCH function to find an ingredient or recipe name.

Surnames have been omitted from photographs out of respect for individual
privacy. Family members and relatives will recognize individuals.

Some recipes omit temperature and baking/cooking times.
These are often commonly known, but if in doubt,
do some online research or consult packaged items in
your pantry or fridge that are similar to the recipe.

Some recipes may specify quantities larger than you are
accustomed to (.e.g. seven pounds of grapes). Remember that
these recipes are from a time when many households had their
own gardens and people preserved food for the midwest Winter.

Readers are encouraged to bring errors to the author's attention
by email to: djkennebeck@emmaus-way.com

Rosa - 3 years old, 1905

Page

Sponge Cake.

1 cup sugar
1 cup flour (heaping)
5 tablespoon milk
2 teaspoon Baking powder
Butter size of a walnut
3 eggs — salt — flavor. lemon

Sugar
Flour
Milk
Butter
Eggs
Salt
Lemon flavor
Baking powder

Layer Cake

1 cup sugar
1/4 cup Shortening
1 cup milk
2 eggs — salt — flavor
2 teaspoon baking powder

Sugar
Milk
Eggs
Flavoring
Shortening
Baking powder

Gertrude 1853-1910 and John 1844-1910, 1871

Sour Cream Cake | Coffee Cake

Sour Cream Cake

1 cup sugar
1 cup sour cream
1 teaspoon soda
2 eggs — salt.
1 cup flour
1 teaspoon nutmeg.

Sugar
Sour cream
Baking soda
Eggs
Salt
Flour
Nutmeg

Coffee Cake

1 cup sugar
1 cup molasses
1 cup shortening
1 cup strong coffee
4 cups flour
1 teaspoon soda
salt — spices.

Sugar
Molasses
Shortening
Strong coffee
Flour
Baking soda
Salt
Favorite spices

Page 2

Catherine 1877-1942 (1888)

Hickory Nut Cake | Devil's Food Cake

Page 30

Hickory Nut Cake

1 cup butter
2 cups sugar
1 cup sweet milk
3 cups flour — salt.
Whites of 7 eggs - yolks of 2
2 teaspoon baking powder
1 pint hickory nuts

Butter
Sugar
Sweet milk
Flour
Salt
Eggs
Baking powder
Hickory nuts

Devil's Food Cake.

1 cup sugar
½ cup shortening
2 eggs
1 cup sour milk
1 teaspoon soda
3 level tablespoon cocoa
2 cups flour (about)
1 teaspoon vanilla — salt

Sugar
Shortening
Eggs
Sour milk
Baking soda
Cocoa
Flour
Vanilla extract
Salt

Peter's Family (1890)

Page 4

Angel Food Cake

1 cup sugar
1⅓ cup flour - ⅓ teas. salt
½ teaspoon cream of tartar
3 teaspoon baking powder
1 teaspoon vanilla or almond
⅔ cups scalded milk.

Mix and sift first five ingredients four times. Add milk very slowly while still hot, beating continually, add flavor, mix well and fold in egg whites beaten until light. Put into greased pan. Bake in a slow oven 45 min. Remove from oven invert pan and allow to stand until cold.

Sugar
Salt
Baking powder
Extract
Milk
Egg white

Elizabeth and Henry's Wedding, 1890

Rich Fruit Cake

Rich Fruit Cake.

1 cup shortening
1 cup sugar — 3 eggs
Whites beaten seperate & stiff.
2 cup seeded raisin
2 cup currants
2 cup flour
1/2 cup shelled almonds
1 tablespoon orange peel
1 tablespoon lemon peel
1 cup sliced citron
1/2 cup grape juice (or wine)
1 teaspoon cinnamon
1/4 teaspoon grated nutmeg
1/4 teaspoon ground mace
1/4 teaspoon allspice
1/4 teaspoon cloves
1/2 teaspoon salt
2 teaspoon baking powder

Sugar
Shortening
Egg white
Raisins
Currants
Flour
Almonds
Orange peel
Lemon peel
Citron
Grape juice
Cinnamon
Nutmeg
Ground mace
Allspice
Cloves
Salt
Baking powder

Catherine and Frank, 1899

Coffee Cake

2 cup flour
2 teaspoon baking powder
2 tablespoon sugar
2 tablespoon shortening melted
3/4 cup milk   salt

Sift dry ingredients, add melted shortening and milk. Spread 1/2 inch thick in greased pan, add top mixture. Bake 30 min. in moderate oven.

Sugar
Flour
Baking powder
Shortening
Salt
Milk

Top Mixture

2 tablespoon flour
1 tablespoon cinnamon
4 tablespoon sugar
4 tablespoon melted shortening

Mix dry ingredients, spread over top of dough before baking.

Flour
Cinnamon
Sugar
Shortening

Frank 1874-1922 (1895)

Children's Sponge Cake | Johnny Cake

Children's Sponge Cake.

1½ cup flour
1 cup sugar — 2 eggs
2 teaspoon baking powder
milk or cream
Beat eggs into a cup and fill
with milk. Beat all together 5 min.

Sugar
Flour
Eggs
Baking powder
Milk/Cream

Johnny Cake

2 cups corn meal
1 cup white flour
2 tablespoon sugar
1 teaspoon soda — salt
2½ cups sweet milk
1 tablespoon soft lard.
Bake ¾ of an hour

Corn meal
Flour
Sugar
Baking soda
Salt
Milk
Lard

Working the farmland (1900)

Spice Cake

Page 8

1 cup sugar
1/2 cup shortening
1 teaspoon cinnamon
1 teaspoon nutmeg
1 cup sour milk
1 teaspoon soda
2 cup flour — salt
1 cup raisin — 1 egg
Bake 40 min. moderate oven.

Sugar
Shortening
Cinnamon
Nutmeg
Sour milk
Baking soda
Salt
Egg

Noname Cake

1 cup sugar — 1 cup molasses
1 tablespoon corn starch
1 1/2 cup sour milk
2 teaspoon soda — salt
1/2 teaspoon each cinnamon, cloves, allspice
3 cup flour

Sugar
Molasses
Corn starch
Sour milk
Baking soda
Salt
Cinnamon
Cloves
Allspice
Flour

John 1862-1928 and Anna 1867-1932 wedding, 1903

Shadow Cake | Pancake Cake

Shadow Cake

2 cups sugar
1/2 cup shortening
1/2 cup sour milk
1 teaspoon cinnamon dissolved in
1/2 cup hot water
1 teaspoon soda
6 tablespoon chocolate
1 teaspoon vanilla — salt
2 heaping cups flour.

Pancake Cake

3 large spoon flour
1 teaspoon soda
1 egg or none — salt
Sour milk until soft dough

Sugar
Shortening
Sour milk
Cinnamon
Baking soda
Cocoa
Vanilla extract
Salt
Flour

Flour
Baking soda
Egg
Salt
Sour milk

Post Card to a relative. Feb. 18 1907; 1 cent postage

Page 10

Buckwheat Cake

2 cup buckwheat flour
1 cup flour
6 teaspoon baking powder
1½ teaspoon salt
2½ cup milk or milk and water
1 tablespoon molasses
1 tablespoon melted shortening

Roll Jelly Cake

1 cup sugar
1 cup flour   salt
6 tablespoon cold water
2 eggs beaten
2 teaspoon baking powder

Bake in a thin sheet turn out on
cloth covered with powdered sugar
spread with Jelly and roll
while hot.

Sugar
Buckwheat flour
Baking powder
Salt
Milk
Molasses
Shortening

Sugar
Flour
Salt
Eggs
Baking powder
Powdered sugar
Jelly

Family Wedding (1910)

Page 11

Food for the Gods.

Beat the yolks of 3 eggs, add 1 cup sugar, stir in 2 cup of raisins cut in small pieces. Sift dry ingredients consisting 1 cup flour — 1 teaspoon baking powder ½ teaspoon salt. Add this to the egg mixture with 1 cup of chopped nuts. Fold in lastly the stiffly beaten egg whites. Bake in a large pan for ½ hr. in a moderate oven. Serve in squares with whipped cream.

Sugar
Eggs
Raisins
Flour
Baking powder
Salt
Chopped nuts
Whipped cream

Lil Rascals (1910)

Crumb Cake

Crumb Cake

Mix thoroughly as for pie
crust ½ cup shortening
1 cup sugar
2 cup flour
1 teaspoon each of cloves,
nutmeg & cinnamon
Set aside ½ cup of this mixture
to the remainder add 1 egg
2 Tablespoon molasses
1 teaspoon soda dissolved in
1 cup of sour milk
Mix well and pour into a greased
pan. Over the top crumble the
1½ cup of mixture. Bake in
a moderate oven 30 minutes

Sugar
Shortening
Flour
Cloves
Nutmeg
Cinnamon
Egg
Molasses
Baking soda
Sour milk

Middle: Rosa - 13 years old, 1915

Page 13

Gingerbread.
½ cup shortening
½ cup sugar — 1 egg
1 cup molasses
1 teaspoon each ginger, cloves
cinnamon ½ teaspoon nutmeg.
1 cup sour milk
1 teaspoon soda
2 cup flour
Mix into a light dough and bake
in a flat pan. Quick oven.

Sugar
Shortening
Egg
Molasses
Ginger
Cloves
Cinnamon
Nutmeg
Sour milk
Baking soda
Flour

Coconut Cake.
1 cup sugar — 2 eggs
½ cup shortening
1½ cup milk & salt
2 cups flour
2 teaspoon baking powder
½ cup coconut.
Flavor in icing mapeline

Sugar
Eggs
Shortening
Milk
Salt
Flour
Baking powder
Coconut
Mapeline

John, 1893-1978 (1915)

Marble Cake

Marble Cake

½ cup shortening
1 cup sugar — 3 eggs
⅔ cup milk
2 cup flour
3 teaspoon baking powder
½ teaspoon flavor

Divide the mixture, leave ½ plain. Into the other half beat 2 level tablespoon cocoa
½ teaspoon cinnamon
¼ teaspoon cloves
¼ teaspoon soda

Put the two mixtures alternately, by a large spoonful into a loaf tin. Do not stir, but smooth over the top. Bake in a slow oven. This Cake does not require icing.

Sugar
Shortening
Eggs
Milk
Baking powder
Flavoring
Cocoa
Cinnamon
Cloves
Baking soda

Ben and Christine, 1916

Page 15

Sunshine Cake

3 tablespoon shortening
3/4 cup sugar
Yolks of 3 eggs
1 teaspoon flavor
1/2 cup milk
1 1/2 cup flour
3 teaspoon baking powder

Bake in greased loaf pan in moderate oven 35 to 45 min.

Ginger Puffs.

1 cup sugar
1/2 cup shortening — 1 egg
1 cup molasses
1 tablespoon ginger
1 teaspoon soda
1 cup water — salt.
3 1/2 cup flour
to be baked in gem molder

Sugar
Shortening
Eggs
Flavoring
Milk
Flour
Baking powder

Sugar
Shortening
Egg
Molasses
Ginger
Baking soda
Salt
Flour

Ben and Christine's 50th, 1966

Apple Sauce Cake

Apple Sauce Cake

1 cup sugar
1/2 cup shortening
2 eggs beaten — salt.
1/2 teaspoon each nutmeg,
cloves, cinnamon, allspice.
Mix 1/2 teaspoon soda and 2
teaspoon baking powder with
1 3/4 cup flour, lastly add
1/2 cup raisins, last 1 cup
slightly sweetened apple
sauce (No milk.)

Apple Sauce Cake

Cream 1 cup sugar, 1/2 cup shortning. Dis
solve 1 teaspoon soda in a little hot water, stir
this in 1 cup sour apple sauce, letting it
foam over into the mixing bowl. Add 1 3/4 flour
sifted with 1 teas cinnamon, 1/2 teas. each
cloves and nutmeg. Mix and then put in 1 cup
raisins. Bake in a loaf tin about 45 min.
This cake is rich & moist, & delicious cake. (No milk
No eggs)

Sugar
Shortening
Eggs
Salt
Nutmeg
Cloves
Cinnamon
Allspice
Baking soda
Baking powder
Raisins
Apple sauce

Peter 1890-1978 and Teresa's 1896-1989 Wedding, 1916
Ben 1891-1970 and Teresa 1898-1974
Herbert 1890-1981 and Otillia 1897-1970
The Flower Girl is Marcella

Prunella Cake

Prunella Cake.

½ cup shortening
1 cup sugar   2 eggs
⅔ cup sour-milk
1⅓ cup flour
⅔ cups stewed prunes
½ teaspoon each of soda, salt,
cinnamon, nutmeg, allspice, baking soda.
Cream shortening, sugar, eggs,
add chopped prunes, stir in
milk, add sift dry-ingredients.
Pour into 2 layer pans, bake in
moderate oven 25 min. Cool.

Creamy Icing

Mix 2 cups powdered sugar, ½ teaspoon
cinnamon, ⅛ teaspoon salt, combine half
with 2 tablespoon ... Add remaining
sugar, 2 tablespoon ... juice, and 1
tablespoon lemon juice. Beat until
creamy.

Sugar
Shortening
Eggs
Sour milk
Flour
Prunes
Baking soda
Salt

Powdered sugar
Cinnamon
Salt
Prune juice
Lemon juice

Teresa and Peter, 1916

Page 25

Icing & Fillings.

Sea Foam Icing

1 cup brown sugar
½ cup water
white of 1 egg
1 teaspoon baking powder

Boil sugar and water without stirring until syrup spins a thread. Add hot syrup slowly to beaten egg white, beating continually. Add baking powder. When icing foams, put between layers and on top of cake.

Brown sugar
Egg white
Baking powder

Chocolate Frosting

2 tablespoons grated chocolate
½ cup water
½ cup sugar
Boil until thick.

Grated chocolate
Sugar

Frank (front left) and Family (1920)

Page 26

Chocolate filling & Icing

Whites of 2 eggs
2 cup confectioners sugar
1½ tablespoons milk
1 teaspoon vanilla
2 ounces unsweetened chocolate
1 teaspoon butter.

Beat whites until stiff, add sugar slowly, beating well, add milk, vanilla and chocolate which has been melted with butter, mix until smooth. Spread on Cake.

Confectionary sugar
Eggs
Milk
Vanilla extract
Unsweetened chocolate
Butter

Helen 1896-1966 and Henry 1893-1960, 1920

Hickory Nut Filling

Page 27

1/2 cup hickory nuts chopped
1/2 cup seeded raisin chopped
1 cup sugar — 1 egg
1/2 cup water — 1/2 tea. butter
1 teaspoon corn starch.
Boil all together for 2 or 3 min.

Cake Filling

1 cup sweet milk
1/2 cup sugar
1 tablespoon corn starch
1 egg — flavor to taste

Sugar
Hickory nuts
Raisins
Egg
Butter
Corn starch

Sweet milk
Sugar
Corn starch
Egg
Flavoring

Joseph, Rosa, Susan, Mary and Louis (1920)

Carmel Filling

1½ cup brown sugar
1 cup sweet milk (or)
½ cup cream
Little Butter — vanilla
Boil 10 minutes

Icing (Radio)

1 cup confectioner's sugar
1 teaspoon vanilla
2 teaspoon boiling water
Mix all together and add 1 teaspoon butter.
Maybe you have to add
another teaspoon of water if
to thick.

Brown sugar
Sweet milk
Cream
Butter
Vanilla extract

Confectionary
sugar
Vanilla extract
Butter

Mary, Rosa and Susan (1920)

Page 35

Pies.

Plain Pastry.

2 cups flour
1/2 teaspoon salt
2 teaspoon baking powder
1/2 cup shortening
8 tablespoon cold water
This make 1 large pie.

Flour
Salt
Baking powder
Shortening

Pie Crust.

1 cup flour
2 tablespoon shortening
3 tablespoon water
Makes 1 pie.

Flour
Shortening

Rosa, Joseph, Susan, Louis, and Mary (1920)

Page 36

Lemon Meringue Pie.

2 cups water
4 tablespoon Corn starch
1 cup sugar — 2 eggs
4 tablespoon lemon juice
1 teaspoon grated lemon rind
1 teaspoon salt

Line Pie Plate loosely with pastry and bake quickly until light brown. Put water on to boil, mix corn starch sugar with little water until smooth, mix in eggs yolks, add slowly to boiling water. Cook 5 min. stirring, add lemon juice, rind and salt. Pour into baked crust. Beat egg whites, add 3 tablespoon sugar, 1 teaspoon baking powder, and spread thickly on top of Pie. Bake in hot oven until light brown.

Salt
Corn starch
Sugar
Eggs
Lemon juice
Lemon rind

Mary 1900-1990 (1920)

Page 37.

Pumpkin Pie.

1 cup sugar
3 tablespoon pumpkin
1 pint milk (if pumpkin is dry)
2 eggs — salt
Spices to taste
1 teaspoon corn starch instead
of 1 egg, if they are scarce.
Makes 1 Pie

Sugar
Pumpkin
Milk
Eggs
Salt
Spices

Buttermilk Pie.

1 cup sugar — 1 egg
1½ cup buttermilk (1½ cup)
1 cup chopped raisins (seeded)
1 teaspoon cinnamon
¼ teaspoon cloves.
Mix all together, and bake
between two crusts.
Makes 1 pie.

Sugar
Egg
Buttermilk
Raisins
Cinnamon
Cloves

A clan (1920)

Page 38

Custard Pie

2 cup milk
1/2 cup sugar   3 eggs
1 teaspoon corn starch
1 teaspoon nutmeg.
    Makes 1 pie.
Coconut Custard is made
the same way, by adding
1/4 cup coconut, instead of
the 1 teaspoon nutmeg.

Sugar
Milk
Eggs
Corn starch
Nutmeg

Cranberry Pie.

1 cup sugar
1 cup chopped cranberries
1 cup boiling water
1 tablespoon corn starch
Little Butter
Cook first
    Makes 1 pie.

Sugar
Cranberries
Corn starch
Butter

Mary, Rosa and Susan (1920)

Page 39

Dutch Apple Pie.

1 cup sugar
1 cup milk — 2 eggs
Fill the unbaked crust with
chopped apples and pour the
cream filling over them, and
beat the whites of the eggs
for over top and then bake.
⊗ Rhubarb Pie can be
made the same way using
rhubarb instead of apples.

Sugar
Milk
Eggs
Apples

Prune Pie.

1 pound prunes
2 cups water
1½ cup sugar
Juice of one lemon
Grated rind of a half a lemon
(Pastry)

Prunes
Sugar
Lemon

Susan 1903-1976 (1921)

Page 408

Mock Mince Pie

1 cup sugar
1 cup bread crumbs
1 cup vinegar
1 cup water
1 cup molasses
½ cup currants
½ cup raisin — salt
Little Butter — Spices

Heat it and then it is ready for two pies.

Recipe for tomato Mince Meat can be found in this book. with recipes for pickels & relish.

Sugar
Bread Crumbs
Vinegar
Molasses
Currants
Raisins
Salt
Butter
Spices

Rosa and Henry, 1923

Chocolate Pie.

Page 41

2 cups milk

½ cup sugar

Bring that to a boil then add

2 tablespoon corn starch

1 tablespoon cocoa

Yolks of two eggs.

Stir with a little cold water then stir into the boiling milk. Then put it in a baked crust. Beat whites of 2 eggs for on tops. If whipped cream is used for on top it can be made without eggs.

Banana or Coconut Cream Pie can be made the same way, instead of cocoa, either use bananas, or coconut. Do not add these until mixture is cooked.

Sugar
Milk
Corn starch
Cocoa
Eggs

Ladies at Rosa and Henry's wedding 1923

Good Old Raisin Pie

Good Old Raisin Pie

1 cup seedless raisin
2 cup boiling water
Juice of ½ lemon or lemon flavor
1 tablespoon flour
¾ cup sugar
1 teaspoon butter.

Cook raisins in boiling water until tender. Mix flour and sugar, add to raisins, stirring until thick. Add lemon and butter, cool slightly and bake between two crusts.

Makes 1 Pie

Sugar
Seedless raisins
Lemon
Flour
Butter

Gents at Rosa and Henry's wedding 1923

Sour Cream Pie

Page 43

Sour Cream Pie

1 cup sour cream
1 cup sugar — 2 eggs
1 cup seedless raisin
1 teaspoon cinnamon
½ teaspoon cloves
1 tablespoon flour
1 tablespoon butter
1 teaspoon vanilla

Put sour cream, sugar, raisins, and spices together let come to a boil, and thicken with the flour and egg yolks which have been added to a little water. Stir well, and boil until thick. Pour in baked crust. Beat whites of 2 eggs stiff add 2 tablespoon sugar. Spread over top and brown

Sugar
Sour cream
Eggs
Seedless raisins
Cinnamon
Cloves
Flour
Butter
Vanilla extract

John, Henry, Rosa, and Mary, 1923

Butterscotch Pie

Butterscotch Pie

1½ cups brown sugar
1½ cups water or milk
1 tablespoon flour
1 tablespoon corn starch
3 tablespoons butter
1 teaspoon vanilla
2 eggs — salt.
Make same like any
other cream pie. Put
Meringue on top.

Brown sugar
Flour
Milk
Butter
Corn starch
Vanilla extract
Salt
Eggs

Mary, Rosa, John and Henry, 1923

Page
50

Molasses Cookies

2 cup molasses
1 cup shortening (melted)
1/2 cup sugar
1/2 cup sour milk
1 teaspoon soda — salt
1 teaspoon each ginger, cloves,
cinnamon

Sugar
Shortening
Molasses
Sour milk
Baking soda
Ginger
Cloves
Cinnamon

Cookies

2 cups sugar
1 cup shortening
1 cup sour milk
1 teaspoon soda
2 teaspoon baking powder
3 eggs — salt
Vanilla and lemon flavor
Flour to make a stiff batter

Sugar
Shortening
Sour milk
Baking Soda
Baking powder
Salt
Vanilla extract
Lemon flavor
Flour

Mary 1900-1990 and Martin 1894-1982, 1925

Page 51

Fruit Cookies

1½ cups sugar
2 cups sour cream
1 cup raisins — 3 eggs
1 cup chopped nuts
1 cup coconut
2 cup rolled oatmeal
2 cups flour
1 teaspoon soda
½ teaspoon salt
1 teaspoon cinnamon

Drop from a teaspoonful unto well greased pan, and bake in a moderate oven.

Sugar
Sour cream
Raisins
Eggs
Nuts
Coconut
Rolled oatmeal
Baking soda
Salt
Cinnamon

Four generations: Catherine S. and Catherine P.
with Rosa holding Bernard Vernon (Vern) 1926

Ginger Snaps | Ginger Drops

Page 52

Ginger Snaps

1 cup sugar
1 cup molasses
1 cup shortening (melted)
1/2 cup hot water — 2 egg
1 1/2 teaspoon soda
1 teaspoon ginger — salt
1/2 teaspoon cloves & cinnamon

Sugar
Molasses
Shortening
Eggs
Baking soda
Salt
Ginger
Cinnamon
Cloves

Ginger Drops

1 cup light brown sugar
2/3 cup shortening
1/2 cup cold water — 1 egg
2/3 cup molasses
1 large tablespoon ginger
1 large teaspoon soda
3 cups flour

Drop by teaspoonful on a well greased pan, bake in moderate oven.

Brown sugar
Shortening
Molasses
Ginger
Baking soda
Flour

Rosa holding Vern (1926)

Page 53.

Raisin Drop Cookies

4 tablespoon shortening
1 cup sugar — 1 egg
2/3 cup milk
1 3/4 cup flour — salt
3 teaspoon baking powder
1 cup raisins
1 teaspoon vanilla

Sugar
Shortening
Milk
Flour
Salt
Baking powder
Raisins
Vanilla extract

Christmas Cookies

2 cup sugar — 2 eggs
1/2 cup shortening
2 cups milk + salt
1 teaspoon nutmeg
4 teaspoon baking powder
Add enough flour to make
a stiff batter.

Eggs
Shortening
Milk
Salt
Nutmeg
Baking powder
Flour

Joe 1905-1983 and Pauline 1908-1999 (seated)
Louis 1908-1990 and Martha, 1931

Page 54

Christmas Rocks.

1 cup shortening
1½ cup sugar — 3 eggs
2½ cups flour
1 teaspoon hot water
¾ lb. chopped dates — cut fine
1½ lb. whole nuts
1 tablespoon cinnamon
½ tablespoon allspice

Mix all to-gether, drop by spoonful on buttered pans, and bake in a quick oven. This makes 8 dozen.

Sugar
Shortening
Eggs
Flour
Dates
Nuts
Cinnamon
Allspice

Joe and Pauline's 50th, 1981

Filled Cookies

3½ cups flour - 1 tea-Vanilla
½ cups shortening
1 cups sugar — 1 egg
2 teaspoon ~~cream of tartar~~
½ cups milk = ½ t. soda

Cream butter & sugar, add beaten
egg, then the milk. Sift the
baking powder into the flour &
stir into the liquid. Knead
into a soft dough, roll into
thin sheets, cut into rounds,
place a teaspoonful of the filling
on one round of the cookie, and
cover with another round. Press
edges of the rounds together and
bake in a hot oven. The hickory
nuts filling on page 27 can be
used for this cookie filling.

Sugar
Flour
Shortening
Vanilla extract
Egg
Cream of tartar
Milk
Baking soda

Henry, Rosa, Elvera and Vern (1932)

Page 56

Oatmeal Cookie (Rose)

2 cups brown sugar
½ cup shortening
½ cup sour milk
1 teaspoon soda - salt
1 teaspoon cinnamon
2 cups flour
2 cups rolled oats
½ cup chopped nuts
½ cup raisin.

Drop by teaspoonfuls on buttered pans. Makes 3 dozen.

Verona 1917-1999 and Alfred 1917-2010, 1940

Date Nut Bars

Page 57

Date Nut Bars.

1 pound dates cut fine
1 cup nut meats
3 eggs beaten seperately
1 cup sugar
1½ cups flour
3 teaspoon baking powder
1 teaspoon vanilla

Put in square pans and bake, cutting immediately. When cool put in bag of powdered sugar and shake. They are better than candy. Put wax paper in pan before baking, so they will not burn.

Sugar
Dates
Nut meats
Eggs
Flour
Baking powder
Vanilla extract
Powdered sugar

Elizabeth 1871-1966 (1940)

Potato Doughnuts

Doughnuts.
Potato Doughnuts.

½ cup milk
1 cup mashed potatoes
3 teaspoon baking powder
½ teaspoon cinnamon
1½ cups sugar
2 tablespoon butter — melted
3 cups flour — 2 eggs
½ teaspoon salt
¼ teaspoon nutmeg
1 teaspoon vanilla

Beat the eggs, add sugar, beat for 2 min. Add potatoes mashed melted butter, milk and all the dry ingredients well mixed, and vanilla. Mix carefully until a soft dough is formed, toss upon a floured board roll out to thickness of ¼ in. Cut and fry in deep fat.

Sugar
Milk
Mashed potatoes
Baking powder
Cinnamon
Butter
Eggs
Flour
Salt
Nutmeg
Vanilla extract
Fat/vegetable oil

Marcella 1908-1992 and Alfred 1909-1978, 1942

Page
62

Doughnuts.

1 cup sugar — 3 eggs
1½ cups sour milk
6 tablespoon shortening (melted)
1 teaspoon nutmeg
1 teaspoon soda
Flour enough to make a stiff
batter Fry in deep fat.

Sugar
Eggs
Shortening
Nutmeg
Baking soda
Flour
Fat/vegetable oil

Vern (1943)

Page 67½

Muffins & Pudding (etc)

Muffins

2 cups flour
3 teaspoons baking powder
1 tablespoon sugar
½ teaspoon salt
1 cup milk — 2 eggs
2 tablespoons shortening.

Graham Muffins

2 cups graham flour
2 cup sweet milk
1 teaspoon soda
2 tablespoon sugar
1 egg — salt
1 tablespoon soft lard
Bake in a hot oven.

Sugar
Flour
Baking powder
Salt
Eggs
Milk
Shortening

Flour
Sweet milk
Baking soda
Sugar
Salt
Egg
Lard

Vern and Elvera (1943)

Graham Pudding

Graham Pudding.

2 cups graham flour
1 cup molasses
1 cup raisins — salt
1 cup sweet milk
1 teaspoon soda.
Steam 3 hours.

Sauce for Pudding

1 cup water
2 tablespoon jelly
1 tablespoon sugar
1 teaspoon corn starch

Put water into sauce pan bring
to a boil, add jelly and sugar
stir until dissolved, add corn
starch which has been dissolved
in a little cold water, boil
3 minutes.

Graham flour
Molasses
Raisins
Salt
Sweet milk
Baking soda

Sugar
Jelly
Corn starch

Vern 1924-2001 and cousin Edwin 1926-2012 (1944)

Bread Pudding | Rice Pudding | Brown Bread

Page 69

Bread Pudding

2 slices bread
1¼ qt. milk
Let this soak, then add
2 eggs beaten
1 teaspoon cinnamon
Raisins may also be added.
Mix all together bake until done

— (Rice Pudding) —

Is made the same as
bread Pudding, instead of
the bread, you can add
1 cup cooked rice. (thick)

Brown Bread

2 cup sour milk
2 cups corn meal - salt.
2 cups flour - 1 teaspoon soda
½ cup molasses
Steam 4 hours.

Sugar
Bread
Milk
Eggs
Cinnamon
Raisins
(Bourbon)

Above but
rice replaces bread

Sour milk
Corn meal
Salt
Flour
Baking soda
Molasses

Henry (1945)

Page 70

Waffles.

2 cup flour
4 teaspoons baking powder
3/4 teaspoon salt
1 3/4 cup milk
2 eggs
1 tablespoon melted shortening

Bake in a well greased hot waffle iron until brown, turn once, serve hot with butter or syrup maple.

Flour
Baking powder
Salt
Milk
Eggs
Shortening

Fritters

1 cup flour
1 1/2 teaspoon baking powder
1/4 teaspoon salt — 1 egg
2/3 cup milk

Fritters should be fried in deep fat.

Fruit Fritters can be made the same, just add any kind of fruit to the batter.

Flour
Baking powder
Salt
Egg
Milk
Fat/vegetable oil

Marcella, Al, Ed and Elizabeth (1945)

Dumplings

Dumplings.

1½ cup water
2 eggs – salt.
Add flour to make thick batter.

Sauce:

6 tablespoon milk or cream
1 tablespoon shortening

When hot pour over dumpling

Salt
Flour
Milk/Cream
Shortening

Rosa, Henry and Elvera (1945)

Page 113

Pickles & Relish etc.

Sacharine Powder Pickles

Wash and dry pickles, fill 8 qts., take 1 teaspoon of whole mixed spices sprinkle in each jar of pickles on top. Then take 1 gallon of vinegar, 1 cup salt, 2 rounding tablespoons of ground mustard and 10¢ worth of sacharine powder. Mix together well and pour over pickles. This makes 8 qts.

Pickles
Mixed spices
Vinegar
Salt
Ground mustard
Saccharine powder
Canning jars

Syrup for Sweet Pickles

For 7 lbs. of fruit take
4 lb. sugar
1 pt. vinegar.
Make any kind of fruits like peaches, pears etc.

Sugar
Vinegar
Canning jars

Rosa and Henry with 1928 Ford (1945)

Page
76

Easy to <u>Make</u> <u>Pickles</u>.

Cucumbers
1 cup dry mustard
1 cup sugar
1 cup salt — vinegar

Wipe cucumbers with damp cloth do not wash. Pack closely in a two gallow jar to within 3 in. from top. On top of pickles put the following mixture, 1 cup sugar, 1 cup salt, 1 cup dried mustard made into a paste with vinegar, Fill the crock with vinegar, and put weight on top. Ready to use after two weeks. These are delicious.

Cucumbers
Sugar
Dry mustard
Salt
Vinegar
Canning jars

Vern (1945)

Corn Relish

Page 77

12 ears sweet corn
1 head cabbage chopped
8 onions — cut fine.
1 bunch celery — cut fine
3 teaspoons ground mustard
1 quart vinegar
2 cups sugar
1 tablespoon salt
Black Pepper to taste.

Boil all to-gether, while hot put in jars and seal-tight.

Corn Beef.

To 100 lbs. of meat - take 8 lbs. salt — 2 lb. sugar and this package to about 5 gallons cold-water. Don't have to boil it or anything.

Sweet corn
cabbage
Onions
Celery
Ground mustard
Vinegar
Sugar
Salt
Black pepper
canning jars

Beef
Salt
Sugar

Ed 1903-1983, Adele 1904-1952, and Elizabeth (1945)

Sweet Corn | Wax Beans

Page 78

Sweet Corn.

9 cups corn
1 cup salt
1 cup sugar
1 pint boiling water

Mix all together and boil 5 min. then put in jar and seal.

Wax Beans.

Take 7 lbs. raw wax beans and add 3 cups salt, and 1 cup sugar. Let stand and stir occasionally until salt is dissolved. Put in jars and seal tight. Before using soak them in water.

Sweet corn
Sugar
Salt
canning jars

Wax beans
Salt
Sugar
canning jars

Home of Vernon, Elvera and David (Jan. 20, 1946)

Tomato Pickles

Tomato Pickles.

Soak in weak brine, over night ½ bu. green tomatoes, drain well. Cook in vinegar till you can stick a fork in, drain. Pack in jars pour over syrup which is boiling hot. Take 4 lbs. sugar, 1 pt. vinegar whole cinnamon or mixed spices.

Sugar
Green tomatoes
Vinegar
Cinnamon or
mixed spices

Carmela (Kay) 1923-2009. and Vern (1948)

Tomato Mincemeat

Tomato Mincemeat

Take 1 peck green tomatoes, chop them fine then drain off all juice. Add as much water as juice drained off and boil. After this add 6 lbs. sugar, 3 lbs. raisins, and 2 tablespoons each of cloves, cinnamon, nutmeg, allspice, and salt. Boil the mixture until well done, then add 1 cupful vinegar. Boil this again for a short time only, then can in usual way. Put in jars while hot, and seal tight.

Sugar
Green tomatoes
Raisins
Cloves
Cinnamon
Nutmeg
Allspice
Salt
Vinegar
Canning jars

David and Elvera (1949)

Tomato Catsup

Tomato Catsup.

One peck of ripe tomatoes, 1 qt. vinegar, 1 cup brown sugar or white, ½ cup salt, 1 teaspoon black pepper, ½ teaspoon red pepper, 1 teaspoon cloves, 2 teaspoons cinnamon, tie spices in a bag, and boil with tomatoes and vinegar. Cook tomatoes and strain through sieve to take out skin & seeds, then add vinegar and spices. Boil until thick. Put in bottles and cork. This make 8 quarts when boiled.

Sugar
Tomatoes
Vinegar
Salt
Black pepper
Red pepper
Cloves
Cinnamon
canning jars

Henry, Rosa, Vern and Kay (1950)

Chili Sauce.

18 ripe tomatoes (scalded) (and peeled)
add:
6 onions chopped
3 hot peppers chopped
2 cups sugar
2½ cups vinegar
2 teaspoons salt
1 teaspoon each of ground cinnamon, allspice, cloves.
Cook until thick about 1½ hrs. Careful not to burn. While hot put in jars and seal tight.

Sugar
Tomatoes
Onions
Hot peppers
Vinegar
Salt
Cinnamon
Allspice
Cloves
Canning jars

Dairy Farm Barn and Silo (1950)

Page 83.

Wines.

Cherry Wine (from Winn's)

8 qts. of cherries, crush and put them in a crock, do not pit them. Pour on 3 qt. boiling water let it stand, six days, till it is through fermenting, till the cherries come to the top. Strain and add 1½ lb. sugar to a quart and let it ferment until it is through. Skim it every day. Put it in a jug.

Sugar
Cherries
Jug

Vern (1950)

Dandelion Wine

Dandelion Wine-

Take one gallon of blossom press down, then put in a gallon of boiling water leave it for 12 hrs. covered then strain it and add water to make 1 gallon, then put in 3 lbs. sugar to a gallon of wine, then set to ferment.

Sugar
Dandelion
blossoms

David's 1st Grade Class (1952)

(Far right, second row)

Dandelion Wine Plus

Dandelion Wine

Take 2 qts. blossoms, 1 gallon boiling water. Let stand 24 hrs. then strain it. Add 3 lemons, 3 oranges, 3 lbs. sugar, 1 lb. raisin cut them or leave whole. To every 5 gallons use 1 cake yeast. Let this stand in a warm place 4 or 5 days, then strain and put in jugs. Keep filled with warm water to the top until through fermenting, then cork.

Sugar
Dandelion blossoms
Lemon
Oranges
Raisins
Yeast
Bottle

Elvera holding William (1956)

Grape Jam

Grape Jam (from Osboro)

7 lbs. grapes
7 lbs sugar
1 lb. seeded raisin
Walnut meats or Hickery
Nuts. Also seperate the
skins from pulp. Boil
like any other jam; put
in jars while hot; and
seal tight.

Sugar
Grapes
Raisins
Canning jars

Sandra, Lawrence, Daniel, Cynthia, William, Mary Ann (1960)

Page 87

Grape Jelly

Wash the bunches thouroughly, remove the fruit from the stems. Put in a kettle and mash them (no water) boil for 10 min. Strain through bag and let it drip. Measure the juice, add 1 cup of sugar to each cup of juice. Bring to a boil, when it starts boiling, boil it rapidly for only 7 minutes. (no longer)

Grapes
Sugar

Earl 1929-2008, Christine 1896-1986,
and Ben 1891-1970, (1964)

Page 93

Candies.

Butter Scotch.

1 cup sugar
1 cup molasses or syrup
½ cup butter
1 tablespoon vinegar
Pinch of soda
Boil until it crisps, in cold water.

Chocolate Carmels

1 lb. powdered sugar
Add a little milk to make it stick together, make balls, then put it to cool. Then melt ¼ lb. chocolate. Then dip balls with a hat pin in the chocolate and put them on wax paper.

Sugar
Molasses
Butter
Vinegar
Baking soda

Powdered sugar
Milk
Chocolate

David, 1966

Divinity

Divinity.

2 cup sugar
½ cup hot water
½ cup corn syrup
Boil until it forms a soft ball in cold water. Beat 1 white of an egg stiff and pour the syrup over and beat it until it begins to thicken. add ⅔ cup hickory nuts.

Sugar
Corn syrup
Egg
Hickory nuts

Candy.

1 cup sugar
2 cups syrup
1 tablespoon vinegar
1 or 2 cups hickory nuts
Little butter — vanilla
Do not put nuts in until it is all done.

Sugar
Corn syrup
Vinegar
Butter
Hickory nuts
Vanilla extract

House on Park St. (1980) with fruit cellar below stoop

Fudge.

Page 95?

1 cup milk or cream
2 cups sugar
¼ cake chocolate (or)
2 tablespoon cocoa
Butter size of a walnut
Cook until it hardens remove from stove and beat until it thickens. Maple flavor.

Sugar
Milk/Cream
Cocoa
Butter
Maple flavoring

Carmels.

1 lb. Brown sugar
1 cup cream — ½ cup butter
Cook until it forms a hard ball in cold water. Pour into well buttered pans and when near cold cut into squares.

Brown sugar
Cream
Butter

ABOUT THE AUTHOR

D.J. Kennebeck grew up in a small midwestern town in northeastern Illinois. He is the third of Rosa and Henry's three children. David and his wife raised three children, who each had three children.

Before retiring, David served in the U.S. Air Force in the Far East, worked in Information Systems for National Cash Register (NCR) and AT&T, and established his own consulting business. He and his wife also operated a handful of businesses, including "Let's Pretend" — a children's theme party and play center that encouraged children to explore the power of their imagination.

David is grateful to Sandie, the family genealogist, for her help identifying individuals and dates. Their ancestors didn't make it easy. His father had the exact same name as his father's first cousin, who was only three years older and lived close by. They are both pictured herein. Other names like Henry, Peter, John, Ben and Teresa occur frequently enough in the family history to cause confusion. Dates within parens are estimated.

David accepts responsibility for any errors that may exist and welcomes corrections. He likes hearing from readers and can be reached at djkennebeck@emmaus-way.com.

The author in childhood

"Back Then"

Average annual income: $4,000. New Car: $1,650. Bread: .16/loaf. Gas: .20/gal. Coffee: .74/pound. New house: $9,525. DJ average: 275. Minimum wage: .75/hr. President: Eisenhower. CHAMPS: Golf: Ben Hogan; Baseball: NY Yankees; Football: Detroit Lions